How to Get Over a Break Up

An Essential Guide for Break Up Survival and Recovery

By Kathleen Rao

Table of Contents

EXCLUSIVE FREE BONUS CONTENT:

✓ FREE eBook revealing the REAL reasons why men lose interest - and how to make him yours for life!

✓ FREE email newsletter series teaching you how to Attract Him, Captivate Him, and Keep Him for Good!

✓ FREE Video divulging a secret method to make ANY MAN settle down, need you intensely, and love you forever!

Visit www.attractandcaptivate.com/bonus to claim this free exclusive bonus content now.

Introduction

I want to thank you for purchasing this book, and I'd like to point out here at the very beginning that this guide applies equally to heartbroken Guys and Gals!

Each of us has definitely experienced the pain of losing someone important even once in our lives. It could be the death of a family member or a dear friend, or separation from a significant other or partner. Either way, no words can ever describe the pain that we have felt when we facing these scenarios. Probably ages ago, some creative, heart-broken jargonaut coined the expression "having your heart ripped out of your chest" to express the excruciating hurt he/she must have suffered after losing the one he/she most loved. This expression is actually the closest depiction to what we feel, which, if taken literally or otherwise, is actually the feeling of dying.

If you're to be asked, "Which is more difficult, physical dying or emotional dying?" what would your answer be? The vast majority would expectedly take the first choice as the more difficult, because when you die, that's the end of it. You won't have the time and opportunity anymore to make things happen or change them. But there are also people who think that emotional pain is already a death sentence, especially if they just have recently parted ways with a partner, which is why they often themselves why they need to continue living on.

This book provides all the answers you need to deal with the hurt of a break-up, and explains why you need to get up and move on. This book also contains proven steps and strategies on how to prepare yourself for a new IMPROVED life – and a new person to spend your forever with – ahead. Also, if you implement these strategies, your ex is guaranteed to regret his/her move to leave you.

Believe it or not, you can and WILL look and feel more Confident, Healthy, and Attractive (and Happier!) than you ever did with your ex. Read on and let's get started!

5

Chapter 1: The Five Stages of Grief

What's your love story? Obviously, everyone would ideally like to have that special someone to create the grandest love story with. All love stories are a mix of laughter and tears, sweetness and bitterness, but at the end of the day, not all of them has a happy, "sugar-and-spice-and-everything-nice" ending.

When you fall deeply in love, you give everything you have to your significant other – trust, loyalty, heart, body and soul. You and your partner try to settle your differences to make the relationship work. You begin testing the waters at first, and eventually, both of you are already eyeing the idea of forever. But not all relationships succeed. There are instances when couples find out that there's nothing more they can do to save the relationship and the best way to stop the continuous build-up of hatred, anger and pain is to finally call it quits and go on with their lives separately. Sometimes there are bits of hints to the upcoming, painful finale. There are also those occasions when the words "Let's break up" or "I can't do this anymore" just hit you out of the blue – no clue, no excuse, no warning whatsoever. Either way, the result is devastating enough to make you reel and ask yourself many times if this is really happening.

The despair you feel after a break-up is comparable to the pain of losing a loved one, which, as the Kübler-Ross model describes, occurs in five emotional stages. The Kübler-Ross model was originally designed by psychiatrist Elisabeth Kübler-Ross, based on the emotions experienced by terminally ill patients and their relatives. Later on, this concept was applied to any scenario that involves a devastating loss of a loved one by any forms, including death, divorce, break-up, drug addiction and alcoholism, tragedy, etc. It was also used to describe the tremendous emotional breakdown of people who lost something very important, like their job, inheritance, or great wealth. Since this book deals particularly with the painful feelings experienced during relationship splits, the five stages of grief shall be discussed in the same light. It is important to be aware of these stages and the feelings that go with each stage in order to determine how you can manage them.

1st Stage: Denial

Denial is a part of a human psychological frame. It's a defense mechanism – a wall that we instinctively construct to protect ourselves from the pain of reality. In break-ups, the denial stage is characterized by the inability of the person (the one who was left behind) to accept and admit to himself/herself that the relationship has finally run its course. Thoughts like "This is not really happening" or "This is just a bad dream and when I wake up, everything will be back to normal", instantly spring to mind. At the back of your mind however, you know that reality is the exact opposite of your hopes and expectations. But you continue to dwell on your make-beliefs, at least until the shock and the pain subside, even a little.

2nd Stage: Anger

The temporary relief of denial eventually wears off and you feel the need to finally face the truth. Simultaneously, extreme feelings of anger directed at the person who initiated the break-up emerge. Anger towards the self also occurs. You blame yourself, thinking that you've been stupid enough to not recognize the tell-tale signs of a foreboding break-up, or you're too in love and weak to go against the wishes of your partner. Anger usually stems from pride or ego, which is hurt by the reality that we can't always control things to go in the way we want them to, especially those that are related to matters of the heart and relationships.

3rd *Stage: Bargaining*

When anger starts to waver, we all try to get back in control by making a deal with the Omnipotent, fate or the person who left us. When suffering from a recent break-up, you start to think that maybe, just maybe, if you do this and that, he/she will return to you, and everything will turn out okay in the end. You start to look for the possible reasons why the inevitable split happened, and think of ways to repair the damages and somehow salvage your relationship with your partner. You might talk to your partner in utter desperation, and beg for him/her to return to you. Let's just say that during this stage, your pride hits an all-time low, and you don't care anymore if it's trampled over, as long as you get the love of your partner back.

4th *Stage: Depression*

If your bargaining stage produced good results, you're lucky (for now at least, until you realize how this desperation may affect your self-esteem within the relationship). But if your desperate pleas fell on deaf ears, then you're doomed to be in the depression stage for as long as you'll allow. At this stage of grief, you'll be so depressed you'll even fail to go through the normal parts of your regular routine. Work becomes a bummer, sleep becomes evasive, and even brushing your teeth feels like climbing Mount Everest. And laundry? - Forget it.

5th Stage: Acceptance

Acceptance is not easy. Sometimes you reach this stage easily, but sometimes you simply don't. More often, the road to acceptance can take a really long while. Acceptance does not necessarily mean that you should feel happy or that you've returned to your normal self. You might still have feelings of sadness, regret or a little bit of anger, but you know for yourself that you're tired of crying and you're ready to continue moving forward in life.

Chapter 2: Positively Dealing with Your Feelings

Each stage of grief is characterized by a mix of negative feelings. People deal with their feelings in various ways. Some people are secretive about what they actually feel, while others feel better and more comfortable talking about their situations with loved ones, a psychological adviser, or members of support groups.

You should understand that emotions, when uncontrolled, can wreak havoc on your life, career, and other relationships. Coping with a loss is never an easy task, no matter how much or often you experience this. There are even instances when people who suffered too much from a break-up end their lives then and there, or do detrimental harm that would ultimately lead to that.

The first thing that you must do after the separation is embrace all those negative feelings – the pain, sadness, anger, resentment – and let them wash over you. Similar to the pain of a physical wound, emotional pain is a part of natural healing. Resisting it is ineffective, and would only prolong the agony. Worse, it can get you stuck, unable and/or not wanting to move forward. So go ahead and cry your heart out. Shout if you want to, but try to do this in your own room and at daytime when the sun is up and shining, lest you want your neighbors and eventually the police, at your door.

Most of the time, the build-up of negative emotions can be so overwhelming, you have to get yourself together and blow off some steam. Anger, for example, can be really dangerous not only to other people but to yourself as well, so don't keep it in. Look for ways to release that boiling rage without resorting to violence against yourself or others. If you have a gym, maybe it's time to install a sandbag or punch bag and purchase a pair of boxing gloves. You can be creative by putting a picture of your former flame on the punch bag (No kidding!), and blast it with your newly acquired boxing and kicking skills. If you don't have a gym, you can just visit one, but you would have to drop the "ex's picture" idea.

If you're the silent and mild type, you can let out all your feelings by writing them in a journal. Pour out on that piece of paper all the trash talk, curses, sad words, regrets and if-only's inside you. This method is specifically advantageous in such cases when nobody is there to comfort you or sympathize with you.

Talking about your painful experiences to other people (particularly those who will surely support you through thick and thin, like your family and friends), is probably the most powerful method of dealing with and managing your feelings after a break-up. These people provide not only the support and love you desperately need, but they can provide advice and share of their own experiences as well. Remember, you're not the only one who's ever suffered a heart-break. Some of your loved ones may have experienced worse, but they were able to get over it and achieve happiness in the end.

Chapter 3: Kissing the Past Goodbye

If you want to move on and appreciate the good things in life might bring you in the future, you must make peace with your past first and say goodbye to it. It doesn't mean that you have to permanently forget about your past. That would be impossible! The past and its life lessons will forever be a part of you. You will not be the same person as you are now if you never had the experiences of the past – both good and bad. Remember the saying "Experience is the best teacher"? Whatever you did in the past defines a wiser and stronger you. But how can you finally say goodbye to your past and move on to the next chapter of your life? Here are some tips:

1. Stop blaming yourself.

During the bargaining and depression stage, you'll naturally blame yourself for the break-up. Maybe you're right. Yes, there are instances when the final straw in a relationship largely originates from one person. But all couple relationships go down the drain as a consequence of the actions of both parties, not just one. Just like what they say, it always takes two to tango. Nobody wants to be involved with somebody with the goal of breaking up and hurting each other in the end. Two people very much in love with each other try their best to meet the needs of one another. Such relationships typically end due to incompatibility in background, philosophies, etc. which, of course, is nobody's fault, and the termination of the relationship is for the best so that you can move on and find someone you're more compatible with!

2. Understand that most relationships will eventually lead to separation.

Being in and out of a relationship is a trial-and-error test of finding your destined lifetime partner. Hence, expect a lot of heartaches and regrets before finally finding The One. Understanding the nature of this process will better prepare you for an ending to a potential love story, which in turn lessens the pain when you're already in that situation. Having this idea at the back of your mind while in a relationship with someone you really, really want to spend your life with also pushes you to give more effort to strengthen the relationship.

3. Never look back in anger.

It's normal to be angry with your partner after a break-up and angrier at yourself for letting such a thing happen. Remember, there are only things in this world that can make the heart not forget – which are love and hate. Between the two, hate invades the larger part of the heart and soul. So after you're done dwelling in the anger stage during the grieving process, move on and don't ever look back. Don't spend any extra time being angry, especially if you come across your ex who seems to be enjoying his/her newfound freedom.

Don't try to hurt your partner for the pain you've gone through by contacting or stalking him/her endlessly, making desperate threats or doing other things that are rather rash and unthinkable. Revenge is a double-edged sword. The more you try to be a pain in the neck for your ex who is obviously

18

doing his/her best to move on, the more you'll get stuck there, looking desperate and still pining for your lost love to come back, which only makes you look unattractive in their eyes, and makes them be even more glad they've left you behind. How would you ever re-establish your lost confidence and self-esteem? All your plans for vengeance that involve negative actions towards your ex can eventually backfire. TRUST THIS TRUTH: You'll be hurting no one in this process but yourself.

4. Throw away any tiny bit of hope that you and your ex will get back together.

Hope is a good thing, but when you're in the process of recovery after a recent break-up, stay away from it as much as possible. Letting go and finally moving on is totally impossible if you cannot let the hope of reuniting with your ex out of your system. As much as possible, avoid any form of communication or friendship with your ex in order to get over him/her easily. Delete him/her from your list of Facebook or Twitter friends and phone contacts, remove all his/her photos in your Facebook accounts, and don't stalk him/her in social media. Simply put, just move on and move forward.

Make your own relationship closure. This might sound cheesy or crazy to some, but creating your own closure in an almost ceremonial or ritualistic way, like writing your last goodbyes to your ex and burning it, will actually do you good.

5. Never forget to handle the practical matters between you and your ex before finally parting ways with them.

Handling a relationship break-up is not purely emotional; it involves practical issues too, particularly if you've cohabited with your ex for a while. You have to decide who will take that pretty cabinet you and your partner bought on your first anniversary, or the cactus plant you won in a couple's game at a county fair. This may be the only time that you're allowed to talk to your ex, but with the utmost formality that you can muster. During these interactions, throw all emotions aside, at least while you're in the process of negotiation. When there's a particular item that both of you want to keep and you can't reach an agreement, consider just letting your ex have it. If you hang on to it, it may just constantly remind you of your ex. And always remember, belongings are just "things" and really don't matter in the end.

Chapter 4: Giving Yourself the Love that You Deserve

When you were still together with your ex, he/she was always there to have your back. Your whole world revolves around him/her; you probably ignored the other people who loved you even before you met your partner. But now, he/she is gone, and you're on your own again. You might think that no one will love you enough and appreciate who you are, but hey, do you think your ex did these when you're still together? Probably not. Maybe at the start, but if he/she really did love and accept everything about you, you won't be having this heart-break in the first place.

When you're hurting, don't hesitate to seek out a person or persons who you can confide in with honesty. Surround yourself with the people who really love you. That includes family and friends. Your ex is not the only person who loved you. There are a lot of people who loved you from the very start and still love you as you are right now. You might not want your family or friends to be nosy about your break-up, but you must understand that they are the only people in this world who will never stop loving and supporting you, especially during the dire stages of recovery that you would have to undergo after parting ways with your ex.

There are also instances where you may need professional advice from a psychologist or any appropriate counseling expert. Don't sneer at this fact or think less of yourself. Break-ups can be quite traumatic, and leave a person in a mentally and emotionally damaged state. In some cases, the damages are irreparable. If you think that your suffering is just too much to handle, even with the help of your family and friends, seek out professional help as soon as possible. You can also join support groups which involve other people whose situations are similar to you. You'll surely feel relieved and encouraged when you find out that there are people like you who feel the same emotional pain (or probably worse), but are trying to get back on their feet again and start a new life. These days, you can even find various types of counseling online via skype or private internet messaging where you never have to leave the privacy of your own room.

More importantly, begin to love yourself more. Treat yourself to all sorts of luxurious pleasures (for at least a short period of time). Get your favorite meal for takeout, get a message, shop for a new outfit, and do things for yourself that you may normally reserve for a special occasion. Remind yourself that you're a beautiful and a wonderful person. Before you can love others, you must give love and importance to yourself first. This will also prepare your heart for that someone who'll finally come along and fulfill the vows of forever with you.

Chapter 5: Starting All Over Again

Break-ups can undermine not only your self-control, but your self-confidence as well. Actually, the recovery process after splitting with your ex is centered on getting your confidence and self-esteem back, and improving them to be better than before. Never forget the things you've learned from your past relationships and break-ups. If you can, remind yourself of such lessons every day, particularly if the split happened just recently. Start living again. After a lot of tears, pains and lessons learned, you have the wisdom, the capability and a lot of opportunities to become a better and stronger person.

Get back to your normal routine. Slowly do the things that you used to do before meeting your ex. Although such activities can also remind you of your former flame, because you probably did them with him/her while you're still in a relationship, these are the things that you love originally and make you feel in control and add pleasure to your life. For instance, if baking has been your forte all your life, give it a try while recuperating from your recent split. Doing so will tell you that although your world is falling apart and everything around seems like a failure, there's still something that you can do with great control and confidence – something that you're really sure about.

Channel your anger, resentment and all negative emotions into doing things that will give positive outcomes. Focus on your career, pursue an academic degree you've wanted to achieve, or become an expert in arts, music or any other fields where you specifically have talents or want to become talented. Be an Achiever, a Goal-Setter and a Hell-

Bent Career Maker. Be driven to succeed at something specific. Doing so will also keep you busy, therefore getting your mind and focus off your ex.

Give more time to yourself. You're hurt and in an excruciating pain which offers no medicine. So you have every right in the world to laze around and do the things that you've wanted to do, but can't due to the restraints of obligation to your work and your partner. Now that you're free from your partner, you are your own boss of your time. Grab a week or two-weeks, take vacation from the office, and visit the Caribbean. Plan a two-day horseback ride in a beautiful mountain town you've never visited before. Visit a spa and relax. Get a new hair-do and shop for new clothes. Do the things that you enjoy. Have more fun!

Never neglect your health, hygiene and personal care. How can you ever make your ex sorry he/she left you if you're gaining weight, or look sickly, unkempt, and totally uncared for? Eat as regularly as possible, even if you're mind, body and stomach are not up for it. But never binge eat. Practice and maintain a balanced, healthy diet. Make a planned out meal plan and stick to it like glue. Munch on more fresh fruit, veggies and nuts. Avoid alcohol, drugs or any substance that can damage your over-all health (and cause you to lose control over your senses – you will need your senses the most now!).

Keep yourself beautiful on the outside. Don't neglect your shampoo, moisturizers, toothpaste and all other tools for keeping your physical appearance healthy and attractive. Get enough sleep and avoid stress at all times. Stress can increase the risks of developing diseases, allergies, heart attack and even cancers. Besides, you already know what stress can do to your skin, face, body and mental health. Cravings for junk foods and unhealthy sweets are triggered by stress.

Beef up those muscles and go get that sexy bod! Attain good health and fitness by hitting the gym regularly. Exercising not only releases stress, but it also takes your mind off other negative thoughts. It also makes you feel good about yourself, especially after just a couple weeks, when you find out that you can easily fit in to that sexy dress you've been drooling over for a very long time now. Do interval cardio exercising for at least a half hour, 3 times a week. And if you're really serious about having a concrete exercise regimen, talk to a fitness trainer right away. Don't forget the physical-mental exercises like yoga or Pilates, which improves both the mind and muscles thru meditation while in difficult positions.

Go outside more and meet new people. Not all men/women are like your ex. The world is a vast, blue ocean. There are more fish of all shapes and sizes outside, so never stop bringing that fishing rod and find yourself a nice catch. If you don't think this is true, do a quick google search on "world population". Your ex is a mere speck in the whole equation, there are so many potential partners to choose from out there! Don't lose the opportunity to recover fast from your break-up and find your Mr./Ms. Right by spending most of your time inside your dark and gloomy room.

Fate can be naughty sometimes. That guy sitting across you in a coffee shop may be your forever. The lady who you opened the door for may be the fated mother of your 3 pretty daughters in the future. You never know the plans of the Universe for you. So if a nice-looking guy/gal asks you out for some coffee and pastries, don't say no.

Don't get into rebound relationships while you're still in the recovery stage. The last thing you need while you're mending a broken heart and self-esteem is another problem and additional confusion brought on by yourself. If you're not yet sure about your feelings, don't jump right into a new relationship immediately after a break-up, particularly if your reasons are for your own selfish purposes, such as to have somebody to cry on or be dependent on, to make your ex jealous, or to put up an "I'm-so-over-you-and-I've-never-been-this-okay" façade in front of your friends and your ex. You're only kidding yourself, and you will not only hurt yourself but you'll also delay your grieving period.

Also, it will be unfair for the other guy/girl who honestly and sincerely likes you. He/She doesn't have anything to do with the issues between you and your ex, so leave him/her out of your drama. Going for a rebound after your split will only make your ex laugh at your apparent desperation, and/or think that he/she made the right decision of dumping you.

Don't go spreading rumors about your ex. That's very immature. Gossiping about your ex's bad habits will harm your image more than his/hers. When you're still together, he/she was honest and comfortable with you that he/she let you see his/her bad and private sides. That's an unwritten and unspoken confidentiality rule between couples, which signifies the deepening trust in a relationship. Choosing when to open your mouth and speak is a sign of maturity and dignity, and others will respect you more for this. Think about how mature it sounds when you can say to someone "He/She is a great person, we just weren't fully compatible so we decided to part ways and move on separately."

Chapter 6: Giving Your Ex the "Victory!" Smile

How can you show your ex that you've totally moved on and he/she should feel sorry for letting you get away? The answer is by improving your confidence about yourself and not even be aware of it. For instance, if you just focus on developing your career or getting a degree or improving your creativity and natural talents, you become unaware of everything but the tasks you have at the moment. Any man/woman becomes more attractive when he/she is driven and focused, and finds success in another arena of their life. Men like women who handle their career with extreme care and intelligence. Women like men who do their job well and exude confidence whatever they do.

Be confident with yourself and stop being clingy. Letting go and moving on, in and of itself will actually give you more confidence. Once you get over the bargaining stage, discontinue any form of communication with your ex. Why? Absence makes the heart grow fonder. You're not the only who'll miss the things you both enjoy doing when you're still together. Your decision to finally cut off any contact with him/her will make him/her wonder about what you're doing right now, or if you're thinking about him/her or why you're not contacting him/her anymore.

Never think of and/or do any revenge scheming that involves abuse or violence. Give that work to the law of karma. What goes around comes around. The best thing to do is accept reality, be mature about it, and remind yourself that this strength and discipline will ultimately make you appear more attractive to your ex and to others. Men/women like their partners to be mature. Your ex is no different. Surely if he/she finds out you're accepting things with maturity and confidence, he/she will feel at least a twinge of regret in his/her heart. Now that's cool! You're getting revenge yet you're not even abusing him/her, seeing him/her or touching him/her. And the funny thing is, this is the MOST EFFECTIVE way to make your ex regret his/her move!

Have fun being single. There are tons of things you didn't have the chance to do when you're still together with your ex. You probably ditched those sexy dresses because your ex-beau didn't like the way they show off your to-die-for womanly qualities. Maybe it's time for you to revamp your closet. Or your ex-girlfriend used to lambaste you for being effortlessly funny to girls – strangers and acquaintances. Buy the best whitening toothpaste and minty mouthwash to give the freshest breath and most irresistible smile of all time.

Let loose, party, and have fun being in the company of a lot of people. When you feel ready and in control of yourself enough to do so, you can drink (if old enough), but don't overdo it. Take pictures of the wonderful evenings and all-night partying you've had while getting over your ex. The social media is a vast cafeteria where friends and friends of friends meet. Your ex will be seething with jealousy and insecurity when he/she finds out that you're having fun as if nothing hurtful happened to you.

Also, make sure that your ex will know that you're actually doing well after a few months of inactivity and God-knows-what. Meet up with common friends and have fun with them as if everything is normal. News have wings, and your bright mood and happy aura will definitely reach your ex's ears from your common friends. This will also make him/her miss hanging out with you together with those common friends.

Conclusion

I hope this book was able to help you get over your break-up and the pain that comes with it. Feeling hopeless, sad, angry and regretful is natural after a relationship split, but you can channel these negative energies into doing things that will help you cope up with the emotional ills, improve your confidence and over-all health, and become more attractive. These are the qualities that will really make your ex regret letting you go. If he/she fell for you when you first met, create a new version of yourself that's even better than who you were then, and you'll not only make your ex miss you like crazy, but you'll be attracting numerous other potential mates, one of which may be much better suited for you and could end up being your Forever.

And remember, all people undergo the pain of losing somebody important. All relationships, if they're not meant to be, end in separation. But all wounds heal, and all things happen for a reason. For instance, a break-up is just another window of opportunity to meet new people and finally find that person you'll spend your forever with. Relationship splits teach us the lessons about pain and life, and about our own tendencies and traits that can never be taught in schools and universities. Break-ups and losing our loved ones bring tears that will definitely make each and every one of us stronger and more mature.

No go out there and strengthen your will and determination to turn all those bad things around and use them for something good. Pray and never lose faith. Embrace the pain and accept reality. Get ready for what's more to come, because life for you does not end with just a break-up. You'll have many more beautiful bright and happy days ahead in the future, and you'll look back with thanks in the end for the lessons along the way. Because next time, you'll surely find the one, and you'll both be able to more easily realize that what you have is for keeps, and you won't let the pain and mistakes of the past relationships destroy your relationship.

Thank you and good luck! Oh also, if you enjoyed this book, please take the time to share your thoughts and post a review on Amazon. It'd be greatly appreciated!

Also, don't forget to visit http://www.attractandcaptivate.com/bonus to download the exclusive free bonus content now!

Printed in Great Britain
by Amazon